Tennis

Tennis Strategies

The 100 Best Ways To Improve Your Tennis Game

By Ace McCloud
Copyright © 2015

Disclaimer

The information provided in this book is designed to provide helpful information on the subjects discussed. This book is not meant to be used, nor should it be used, to diagnose or treat any medical condition. For diagnosis or treatment of any medical problem, consult your own physician. The publisher and author are not responsible for any specific health or allergy needs that may require medical supervision and are not liable for any damages or negative consequences from any treatment, action, application or preparation, to any person reading or following the information in this book. Any references included are provided for informational purposes only. Readers should be aware that any websites or links listed in this book may change.

Table of Contents

Be sure to check out my website for all my Books and Audio books.

www.AcesEbooks.com

Introduction

I want to thank you and congratulate you for buying this book, "Tennis: Tennis Strategies: The 100 Best Ways to Improve Your Tennis Game." Becoming great at tennis is a task that takes some time and effort. Not everyone is going to have the skills, work ethic and patience in order to be the best. But if you are one of those people who love the game and do not mind putting in the work that it takes to be great, then this is book for you.

Inside the following pages you will discover many basic and more advanced strategies that you can use to perfect your game. Unlike many other players who waste their time practicing things they already know or techniques that everyone else is doing, you will learn advanced skills that can give you a huge advantage over the competition.

No matter the current level of your tennis game, there is always room to improve. In the first few chapters you will learn about powerful mental strategies that can help you stay focused, calm and at the top of your game. You will also learn about proper nutrition and great exercise routines so that you are at your best physically. Once you have that down, you will discover strategies that are based on your specific style of play.

The last few chapters are full of great advice that all tennis players can follow. There is also information on how to be successful during the playing season and in the off-season as well. By preparing during the off-season you will be much more effective when it is game time! There is so much to learn about the game of tennis and having the right strategies available at your disposal, along with a lot of practice, will ensure that you have the leg up on the competition. By utilizing the strategies and techniques you are about to discover, you will be a ferocious competitor on the court of play.

Chapter 1: Mental Strategies

Learning the strategies that work well for your tennis playing style isn't always easy. This is why it is smart to do your research so that you waste as little of your precious time as possible. The mental portion of the game is vitally important to the success of any top athlete. Here are some of the mental strategies you can use in order to master the game of tennis.

Visualize the ball. Yes, you have spent a lot of time on the court playing with the ball and hitting it around, but take a minute to just think about the ball. Imagine that you are watching a video of yourself moving with the ball. Visualize yourself in the third person, as if from a video camera about twenty feet away, and see yourself doing your favorite moves and performing flawlessly. The more that you do this, the better you are likely to perform when this situation arises on the game court. Before each match or practice, take ten minutes to do your visualization. This is a powerful strategy that can greatly improve your performance if done consistently. If you are learning a new technique, be sure to visualize yourself doing it over and over.

Relax and be calm. It is normal to be nervous before you get to a match or a performance. However, this is something that can mess with your thinking and make it difficult to calm down and play at your very best. Learning some relaxation techniques to use before a match can really help you to perform better. Deep breathing is the most common and effective way to calm down before a tense situation. Breathe deeply and purposefully and count to ten. If your heart is beating swiftly and you feel tense, you need to relax. Start at the neck and force your muscles to let go and relax little by little all the way down to your feet.

Focus on your goals. Before practicing your new techniques, you need to have some goals in mind. These will help you to figure out how hard you need to work and what skills will be the easiest to work on next. You should pick some goals that are not impossible to reach but that still require you to put in some effort in order to succeed. Making them too easy to reach might mean that you will not work hard. Making them too difficult sets you up for failure. You may want to work on building up your cardio, serving, forehand, backhand or anything else that you think will help your game play. When making your goals, I have found it helpful to start the goal is with the words: "I will easily..." For example: "I will easily run 1 extra mile per day in order to build up my cardio endurance."

Set and Achieve Small Goals. By setting and achieving small goals, you can build your confidence up to the point where you feel ready and able to take on bigger and more long-term goals. If you are trying to accomplish a long-term goal, like winning the championship, break it down into smaller goals like winning tonight's match, so it seems a lot easier to deal with.

Concentration. During the big match, lots of things could distract you. You could hear the fans, get distracted by the opposing players, get distracted by your own thoughts, or a million other things. You must learn how to overcome the distractions and just concentrate on the match and position you are playing. One of the best ways to do this is to have a pre-match ritual that puts you in the right frame of mind for the match. This ritual can include visualization, your favorite music, memories of past victories, going over your goals or anything else that will help focus you and motivate you to get in the "zone."

Avoid Comparisons. It is easy to compare yourself to others and think how badly you may play compared to them. Get these thoughts out of your head right now. This is a distraction to your game and could be what is getting in the way of you playing your best. It is always better to focus on your strengths and what you can do well rather than comparing yourself to others.

"Stop" Negative Thoughts. Learn how to become more aware of when you start thinking negatively and then say, "stop," either out loud or internally. Many therapists use this technique and you can do it yourself, anywhere. Stopping negative thoughts can prevent you from getting too wrapped up in negative emotions that can bring down your self-confidence. To learn some awesome and easy do-it-yourself techniques on how to stop thinking negatively, I invite you to check out this YouTube video by Nathaniel Solace about Negative Thoughts: How to Stop Negative Thoughts, Fear, Stress, and Self Doubt.

Get to Know Yourself. Knowing yourself and what you like is a major way to become more confident. When you know yourself, what you want, what you like, where you want to be, etc., you can have a better sense of control over your life. A good way to get to know yourself better is to engage in some alone time. It may be a good idea may be to start a journal where you can pour out your deepest thoughts.

Be Optimistic. Have you ever heard that "Attitude is everything?" People who have negative attitudes tend to be followed by negative actions and consequences. People who have optimistic and positive attitudes are more likely to realize their dreams and success. By simply having a positive outlook on life, your chances of living a fulfilling life increase. For example, say that your friend worked a high-paying job and you worked a minimum wage job. If you constantly mope and wallow over the fact that your friend makes more money than you, you will be too busy to figure out how to improve your own paycheck. Studies have shown that optimistic people have a much higher chance of spotting opportunities and capitalizing on them than pessimistic people.

Listen to Your Gut. While you shouldn't let your instincts control you completely, it is often a good idea to at least listen to them. Can you think back to a time where you had a "gut" feeling about something and it turned out that you were right? When you are faced with making a choice, take a few moments to ask yourself what your reasoning is for making that choice. Question your thoughts and feelings before saying yes or no. Taking a few minutes to reflect on your instinct can make all the difference.

8

Learn to Handle Rejection. Having to deal with rejection is inevitable because, at one point or another, you will probably be turned down. whether you're rejected from a sports team, a college, a position, or anything else. Many people tend to let rejection discourage them, but if you can see it in a positive light, you can be much better off for the next opportunity. If you are rejected for something, view it as an opportunity to see what you can improve upon. Also, don't get emotional if someone gives you criticism. They are usually just trying to help and, if you can learn to take criticism without blowing your lid, then you will be much better off in your journey through life.

Resist Fear. Fear is a natural emotion, but many people allow it to control their lives. It is normal to be scared to take risks in your life but sometimes you can deny yourself a great opportunity if you don't try. Learning how to resist fear can open many potential doors for your future. One great way to resist fear is to think about exactly what is holding you back and work on that specific fear. Even over a thousand years ago people knew that fortune favors the brave.

Learn From Your Mistakes. You can't learn unless you make mistakes. Many people allow their mistakes to discourage them but if you can view them as learning experiences, you will always gain personal growth. The key is to learn from your mistakes the first time. For example, if you neglect to brush your teeth and have to spend thousands of dollars on dental work, you should learn from that and begin to take better care of your teeth so it doesn't happen again. Even better than learning from your mistakes is to seek the advice of a mentor or read a good book on the subject you're currently interested in. Avoiding mistakes by taking the advice of others is the best route to take.

Follow the 80/20 Rule. The 80/20 rule is a well-known theory that suggests a great way for people to stay productive. The idea is that you want to focus on the most important 20% of a task that produces the best results and mostly ignore the other 80%. If you follow this rule, you will end up getting much better results. For example, if you score most of your points from a certain point on the court, you should spend the majority of your time trying to get yourself in that portion of the court to score.

Practice S.M.A.R.T. Before you try to tackle a bunch of tasks at once, ask yourself if each one is specific, measurable, attainable, relevant, and timely (S.M.A.R.T). If the answer is "no," you might want to put that task off until a later date. Getting into the habit of focusing your tasks with this acronym can save you a lot of time.

Encourage Others to Succeed. Many people tend to respect those who push others to succeed; it shows that you're not conceited, arrogant, or selfish. It also supports a sense of teaching and mentoring, which can always benefit people and help others improve upon themselves. In a world where many people tend to be selfish, encouraging others to succeed can be fulfilling and could even help change the world.

Team Up With Confident Friends. When you surround yourself with other people who are highly confident, your chances of feeling more confident increase. By surrounding yourself with other confident people, your chances of being surrounded by negative thoughts can also dramatically decrease because there will be less judgment and jealousy around you.

Believe in Yourself. One of the biggest issues with those who do not succeed is that they do not believe in themselves. They do not think that they are as good as everyone else or that they are able to do something as well as others. With enough practice and a bit of confidence, you can do anything that anyone else is able to do. Have faith in yourself and you will be amazed at how far you can go. Some of the most successful people in history weren't the smartest or most talented people; they are people with a strong desire and a good work ethic. If you do something enough times you are bound to become an expert at it. As long as you never give up, you are bound to succeed.

How to Turn Important Activities into Habits

Stay Consistent. Consistency is key when trying to learn a new habit. If you do not practice it every day, or at least a few times a week, you risk the chance of not solidifying the habit. For example, if you want to make it a habit to brush your teeth every morning when you wake up, it will not become a habit if you only do it whenever you feel like it. You must use some willpower and determination to get up every morning and make yourself head straight to the sink. By doing it every morning, you will soon begin to do it on "autopilot."

Write About It. When you write something down, you are more likely to remember it or at least keep it in the back of your mind. By writing down your goal to develop a habit or habits, it can be easier to remember to pursue the change actively. You can also always refer to your notes when you are feeling tempted to give up. It is good idea is to keep a habit-forming journal. You can write about your progress and your thoughts on forming new habits, which can be very inspirational. If you don't want to keep a journal, at the very least have your goals written down on a piece of paper and then try and review those goals daily.

Visualize. Visualization is a powerful habit-forming technique. If you have ever read about goal-setting, you have probably heard about the power of visualizing yourself achieving your goals. Learning a habit is no different, because it *is* a goal. By thinking about what your life will be like once you've learned a new habit, you can feel more inspired and excited to reach the end. Since visualization is such a powerful and important strategy, check out this YouTube video by Howdini titled: <u>How To Visualize Your Goals</u>. Another good strategy is to visualize yourself or the scenario in the 3rd person. In other words, try to pretend like you are observing yourself accomplishing a particular goal or doing the desired task from a distance. Studies have shown that this increases the power of your visualization. While it is important to visualize the desired result, doing this too often can actually be a bit demotivating, as it tricks your brain into thinking the goal has already been achieved. So be sure to also visualize yourself doing the necessary steps in order to achieve your desired goal. For example, if your goal is to win a local race, besides visualizing yourself crossing the finish line in first, be sure to visualize yourself from a distance away running every day, training every day, eating healthy, and whatever other things you deem necessary to achieve this goal.

Pick a Role Model. Sometimes it is not easy to make a change in your life on your own. People often become easily discouraged or think that they cannot do it. One good way to stay focused is to pick a role model. Your role model does not have to be a person who has successfully learned the same habit that you're trying to learn; he or she can be someone who has overcome obstacles in order to achieve success. For example, the builder of the Brooklyn Bridge was told he could never do it and, although he was never even got injured on the job, he still built the bridge and it stands today. Since his story is inspirational, it can serve as a message to say, "Don't give up!"

Eliminate Temptations. To learn a new habit better, get rid of anything that will stop you from achieving your goal. As you probably know, it is very easy to give into temptation. You may give in with the mindset of, "it's only this one time," but many people lose track of how many times they give into temptation and it ends up negatively affecting their progress. So, when trying to learn a new habit, see if there is any way to eliminate temptations in your life. For example, if you're trying to form a habit of eating better, don't keep junk food in your house.

Substitute an Activity. If you are trying to break a bad habit, it can be easier to replace that habit with a new one than to focus on simply stopping the "bad" habit. For example, if you're trying to quit smoking but you're used to smoking while you watch TV, find something else to do as you watch TV. You could chew gum, drink water, massage yourself, or find another way to distract yourself. This way, your mind will not be clouded with the thoughts of smoking.

Develop a Trigger. If you've ever taken a basic psychology class, you've probably heard of triggers before. A trigger sends a signal to your brain telling it to do something. While we tend to think of triggers as bad things, you can also create a trigger to help you stick to learning a new habit. For example, if you want to stop biting your nails, clap your hands together whenever you feel the urge to bite your nails. When you clap your hands and refrain from biting your nails, your brain will eventually learn to associate clapping with no nail biting.

Do it With a Friend. Similar to picking a role model, if you have a friend who wants to learn the same new habit or change the same bad habit, do it together.

Doing things with friends is always fun and easier. It also gives you both the opportunity to motivate each other towards success.

Use Reminders. Sometimes your life may get so busy and hectic that all you need is a reminder to stick to a new habit. In this day and age, setting reminders is easy. You can use post-it notes, set an alarm on your cell phone with a memo, or keep a planner. One good technique is to align your reminders with places or times where you would need to practice your new habit the most. For example, if you're giving up junk food, it would make sense to keep a note on your fridge reminding you that you're trying to eat more fruits and vegetables.

Don't Give Up. One of the most important techniques is to never give up. It's easy to say "forget it," and give up on trying to learn a new habit altogether. However, as long as you practice most of the other strategies, it will be harder to give up because you've invested so much time and effort. Again, visualize the end results and think about how much better your life will be once you've successfully implemented the new habit.

Start Small. One of the biggest mistakes that people make when trying to learn a new habit is trying to make too big a change at the beginning or making too many changes at once. Starting out big or overwhelmed will not get you anywhere and will more than likely stress you out to the point where you'll just say, "Forget it." The key is to start small and take one step at a time. For example, say you wanted to change your eating habits, your thinking habits, and your spending habits. Instead of trying to change all three at once, pick one and work on it until you're where you want to be. Then, pick another one, do the same, and so on.

Reward Yourself. Finally, do not be afraid to reward yourself for successfully learning a new habit! By rewarding yourself, you can give yourself something nice for all the hard work and effort you put into learning the new habit; you deserve it because changes are it wasn't easy! Knowing that you will get a reward at the end also gives you something to look forward to, adding to your motivation.

How Long Does It Take?

Depending on the way you learn, not all of these habit-learning strategies will work for you. Once you decide which of these strategies you would like to use, try it for a while and then ask yourself another important question: "How is this strategy working for me?"

Again, there is no concrete answer as to how long you should spend trying to learn a habit or habit-developing strategy. Some people claim that you can learn a habit within 21 days. Others claim it takes a month and a few more claim that it can take a month and a half. To get the best results, you should spend as much or as little time as you need learning how to master both habit-learning strategies and habits themselves., A good way to control your time is to occasionally pause and ask yourself, "How is this working out for me?" If your strategy is working for you- great! Keep going and continue to reap the rewards from your good habit. If it isn't working out for you or if you're not seeing any progress, then go back to the list and try another strategy until you find one that fits you.

Be sure to take some time now to make some goals, if you haven't already. Once you have your goals, finish reading this book and determine the activities that are most important for you to improve your tennis game. Take those activities and turn them into daily habits.

Chapter 2: Nutritional Strategies

Before you go out and try out some of the techniques to improve your game, you need to make sure that you are fueling your body with healthy food that will give you lots of energy. Too many players tend to rush and skip breakfast when they head out the door or to make poor food choices that do not provide the nutrients that their bodies need in order to be the fighting machines that they want to be on the court. Here are some great tips for eating correctly in order to improve your performance.

Eating Carbohydrates. When you in the middle of a hard practice or you want to have the energy to keep going for a long match, you will need to load up on carbs. These are a great source of energy that will keep your muscles working hard much longer than other forms of energy. Spaghetti and other pastas are great choices. Pick the whole grain varieties because they will break down more slowly and the energy will last longer. You don't want to stuff yourself. It is much better to have more, smaller meals throughout the day then to have fewer large meals, as the larger meals are harder to digest and can slow you down, while smaller meals are easier to digest and help keep you mentally sharp.

Eating protein. Protein is important to the body because it helps to rebuild and repair the muscles that become damaged with exercise. Running around the tennis court can damage your muscles, and without the proper amount of protein in your diet, they might not be able to repair themselves. Some good sources of protein are beans, chicken, eggs, lean beef, milk, cheese, yogurt and protein shakes. My favorite protein drink of all time is Muscle Milk.

Eating fat. Yes, you do need to eat some fat to stay healthy, but you should stick with the healthier options. Choose those that are monounsaturated fats rather than the trans or saturated fats. These are better for your body because they protect the heart while maintaining your cholesterol levels. Some foods with high levels of healthy fats are Salmon, eggs, nuts, avocados, bacon, fatty cheeses, cod fish, liver oil and many others.

Calcium. One nutrient you should include in your diet while training is plenty of calcium. In addition to keeping your bones healthy and strong so they can keep going no matter how hard practice is, calcium is good for the health and the contraction ability of your muscles. Without plenty of calcium in your diet, your muscles might tense up and get sore more easily.

Eat three meals a day and snacks. You should eat at least this much each day for the optimal health. This makes sure that you are getting the right nutrients spread throughout your day rather than falling short at some point. It is best to split your plate up so that it is 2/3 full of vegetables, fruits, and whole grains, and 1/3 full of dairy, beans, and other foods with lots of protein. Almonds are also a great snack and provide lots of energy.

Stay away from fast food and sugar. These are just empty calories that can harm your body. You might get a burst of energy, but it will not last long. Soon you will be lagging on the court and running on empty even if you had enjoyed a big meal while you were eating out. Stay with the healthier options for the best results in your game.

Fruits and Vegetables. These two food groups should become your best friends during training. Without them, you will never get the nutrition that your body needs to perform at its peak. Eat some of each with all of your meals and include them in your snacks every day. I know you have heard this a million times, but seriously start eating more fruits and vegetables... especially vegetables. You will have a lot more energy and be more mentally sharp as well.

Eat Enough Calories. Training is going to be tough on your body and not eating enough calories will make it difficult to keep up and put in the energy that you need for a good practice to use. Pick foods that are high in nutrients and do not skip meals, especially when you are training hard.

Get Enough Sleep. This might not be a nutritional fact, but you should still make sure that you are getting enough sleep while you are training. It does not matter how hard you train, you will not be very successful if you are not giving your body the rest that it needs to recharge. Get at least 8-9 hours of sleep to make sure that you are not undoing all your hard work. This is another critical factor that should not be ignored. If I listed all the side effects from not getting enough sleep it would fill up the next full page.

Multivitamins. Getting enough nutrition when you are working hard during training can be hard. Consider taking a safe and effective multivitamin to help fill in the gaps in your diet. While getting the nutrition from food is the best choice, a multivitamin can help out during training. My favorite multi vitamins are: Opti-Men and Opti-Women.

Stay Away From Caffeine. For long-term success, you are much better off having a caffeine-free life. I have personally tried almost every possible strategy to be successful with caffeine, and the bottom line is that it can give short-term success at the expense of long term success. I won't go into huge details on this, as the harmful effects of caffeine are well known. I could never work out a good long-term strategy for using caffeine and, ever since I quit using it, I have performed much better. I would highly recommend not using caffeine and instead using herbs and supplements instead like: Gingko Bilobo, Gotu Kola, Bee Caps or Focus Formula.

10 Foods all Tennis Players Should Eat

As a tennis player, keeping your body in good form is critical. In addition to the exercise that you should be doing and the drills you need practice, you need proper nutrition to keep your body going. These foods will provide the nutrients and energy that you need in order to keep you going through the long match. Here are the ten best foods that you can eat before playing or practice:

1. **Complex Carbs**. This would include things like cereals, potatoes, pasta, bread, and rice. Eat them in their whole wheat or whole grain forms for the best results. Loading up on carbs before a big match or practice can help you to play longer and have the energy that you need to keep going.

2. **Vegetables**. You can never eat too many vegetables during the season. You will deplete a lot of your nutrients by running around on the court but eating plenty of vegetables before and after the match can help greatly.

3. **Fruits**. Make sure to eat plenty of fruits as well. They are another complex carb that can keep your energy level high for a long time.

4. **Eggs**. Eggs provide a great way to get the protein that the body needs to keep on going. Start the morning with a few before going to practice or getting ready for a big match.

5. **Oatmeal**. Since you need to eat breakfast every day to get the energy you need, why not fill your body with something that is wholesome and delicious? Oatmeal is full of complex carbs and so will give you the energy that you need to make it through the big match.

6. **Turkey and chicken**. These are lean sources of meat that will help you get the protein athletes need without all of the added calories or fat. Make sure to get rid of the skin or choose skinless options in order to avoid any extra fat.

7. **Lean beef**. Beef is fine as long as you get the lean varieties. Regular varieties come with a lot of added fat and cholesterol that can harm your health. Choose the lean options to get the protein you need to stay healthy.

8. **Beans**. Pick beans that are low in sodium and do not come in sauces. Black beans are a good option because they provide both the good carbs and protein that your body needs to stay healthy.

9. **Sweet potatoes**. Sweet potatoes are known to cause a big spike in insulin that helps to drive nutrients such as protein to your muscles. This can help you to stay energized through a long match or workout.

10. **Milk**. Drinking milk a few times a day is a good way to pack a lot of nutrients into a meal. If you pick the low fat or skim variety, you will be giving your body lots of good nutrients, such as calcium, as well as avoiding the extra fat. It is good for you all around.

For a complete understanding of how to optimize your health, be sure to check out my bestselling book: Ultimate Health Secrets.

Chapter 3: The Grip

The Importance of The Grip

A fundamental characteristic of tennis is that it requires players to manipulate the ball without ever touching it directly. Like all racquet sports, tennis requires the use of a piece of additional equipment to hit the ball.

Needless to say, because the racquet is the thing that makes contact with the ball, it is a crucial aspect of tennis. There is a great deal that can be discussed about choosing the right racquet. There is perhaps even more to say about the size and type of frame and the tension of the strings. The size and form of the physical grip are also important considerations.

Concerns relating to equipment are beyond the scope of this book. However, all tennis players should choose their tennis equipment carefully and consult an expert before purchasing to ensure they have exactly the right racquet for them.

This chapter discusses the grip, not the physical part of the racquet, but the position of the hands holding the racquet. This is the only connection you have with the racquet and, by extension, the ball. If your grip is incorrect but feels correct to you, then no matter how good the rest of your game, you will always have problems.

The grip is hugely important and it is vital to spend some time getting it right. A good grip on the racquet is the basis of a good stroke and a good tennis game. The position of your hand dictates how the racquet will move through your stroke and decide the type of contact you are able to make on the ball. The angle of the racquet face when it strikes the ball--so crucial for the shape of the shot--is controlled by the way you grip the racquet. Your ability to place a shot where you like, with the desired angle of elevation and the pace and spin you want, is dependent to a huge degree on the grip you use.

There is no one-size-fits-all, perfect grip. It would be easy to recommend one grip for everyone, all the time. But the fact is there are a range of grips to choose from that may suit different people for different shots.

Each grip has a range of pros and cons. To really decide which grip is best for you and when requires a period of experimentation and practice. Once you have tried the different grips and played a range of strokes with them, it will become quite clear that different grips are more suited to particular game situations and different shots.

The angle at which you present the racquet to the tennis ball has a fundamental effect on the shot you will be able to make. The different grips all present the racquet face at a slightly different angle. When the racquet is tilted upwards, this is referred to as an "open" face. When it is tilted downwards, it is known as "closed."

Presenting a "closed" or "open" racquet face affects the point in the stroke at which you should be aiming to make contact with the ball. When your grip creates a closed face, you need to strike the ball further through the stroke so that the racquet is out in front of your body and higher up. A square or more open face will mean that you will hit the ball squarer and lower down.

Considering these facts, the committed tennis player needs to pursue three courses of action. First, they need to be aware of the different options for gripping the racquet and be open-minded about which ones may be best for them. Second, they must be prepared to put in the extra practice in order to try out different grips and give each one enough time to appreciate how they are different and how they can be used. This is actually quite a difficult task and many budding tennis players shy away from it because are reluctant to put in the required time and effort. Playing with a different grip can be quite difficult, uncomfortable, and, at times, can seem as if you are learning to play all the shots all over again. Rest assured that this time and effort will be worth it in the end. Third, to be the very best tennis player you can be will mean having the ability to switch grips between shots. This is no easy skill to master and is not something that beginners need to learn. However, tennis is a competitive sport and if your opponent is able to change their grip to maximize their ability to make shots, they will have a considerable advantage over you.

The purpose of this chapter is to help you place your hand correctly for each of the different grips and to be aware of the different uses of each grip and how they can help improve your shot making and overall tennis game.

How to find the grip. In describing how to locate the grips, the clearest is to start with the base knuckle of the index finger and use it as a key reference point. You should then view the base of the grip where the plastic cap is affixed, enabling you to see the eight sides of the grip. These are composed of four main 'square' sides and an additional four diagonal bevels that link them.

Place the racquet so that the head is vertical. This will give you a top, right, bottom and left side. It will also give you four bevels, with number one between the top and the right sides and proceeding around clockwise.

Using these references, we will now go through the seven main grips. This may seem like quite a lot and even might appear to be unnecessarily complicating the simple act of holding onto the racquet, but do not despair or be intimidated. Instead, consider these seven ways to improve your game and remember that all professional players have experimented with all of these and have used them to make their games world-class.

1. Continental Grip: The Continental Grip might be termed the "traditional" grip. It is also perhaps the most multipurpose of all grips as it can be used for a whole range of shots. As well as ground strokes, the Continental grips allows you to play serves, volleys, overheads and slices, as well as reacting quickly to defensive shots.

You can adopt the Continental Grip by placing your index finger's base knuckle on the first bevel. If you are right-handed, you will naturally form the V of the thumb and your forefinger across the very top of the grip.

+ This is the most natural grip for hitting a serve or an overhead and most players use it for these shots. The Continental grip gives you a good hand position for your forearm and wrist to naturally come through the strike zone. This enables you to generate more power with added flexibility, whilst reducing any strain on your arm.

Moreover, the Continental Grip is also perfect for volleying. This grip opens the racquet face a degree and promotes backspin, which helps you to control your shots. It also has the considerable advantage of being appropriate for both forehand and backhand volleys. When volleying at the net, quick hands are essential and it is important to be able switch quickly between either side.

As was noted above, the angle at which you bring the racquet face through the ball determines the spin and elevation you create. When using the Continental Grip, the racquet is quite square, enabling you to play shots more easily when you receive the ball much lower down and further back. Such an ability is advantageous when you have to play the shot down by your feet and have little time to react. This will be the case when you are playing defensive tennis.

- While it is technically possible to put topspin onto a ball with the Continental Grip, it is not at all easy. Instead, you are much more likely to hit the ball 'flat' or play it with a degree of slice.

This can be a serious disadvantage for groundstrokes, particularly if you want to play attacking shots. Without topspin, you must play your shots much closer to the top of the net, otherwise you are likely to be unable to get the ball back down in time for it to remain in play. This makes playing ground shots much more difficult and considerably increases the chance of error.

2. Eastern Forehand Grip: The Eastern Forehand Grip might be considered the most natural grip. ,This is probably how anyone picking up a tennis racquet without instruction or training would find themselves holding the racquet. For that reason, it is also considered the easiest grip to use.

To locate the Eastern Forehand Grip, it is easiest to begin at the Continental Grip. You should then move your hand around clockwise (if you are right handed). From here, slide the base knuckle of your index finger around so that it is on the right side of the grip. The V of your thumb and forefinger will be over the first bevel.

You should find this quite a natural position for your hand. Indeed, you should be able to pick up the racquet with your eyes closed and find you have adopted the grip correctly. Players who utilize the Eastern Forehand Grip often say that it seems as if you are "shaking hands" with the racquet.

+ As the name suggests, the Eastern Forehand Grip is strongly related to playing the forehand shot. This is a direct result of the position of the hand. When we "shake hands" with the racquet, we are putting our hand, wrist and arm in a strong position for lateral movement. As such, it is ideal for those forehand passing shots, which can be hit "flat" when looking to beat an opponent with speed. Moreover, the Eastern Forehand Grip does allow the possibility of imparting topspin on the ball by easily adjusting the angle of the strike through the ball. This allows more control of forehand ground strokes.

Another advantage is that the Eastern Forehand Grip is a very versatile position. The hand position is almost in the "middle" of the other grips. This means that players are able to shift between other grips more suited to backhands or volleys,, at a moment's notice.

- Of course, the Eastern Forehand Grip also has some disadvantages. It must be remembered that, compared to the Continental Grip, the player is required to strike the ball a little higher and further forward.

However, this far from the best grip for putting topspin on the ball and, as a consequence, is not the best choice for those players hoping to continue long points in which the object is to pin their opponent back on the baseline. The flatter stroke has a high risk of hitting the net. It is also not the ideal grip for trying to return high balls.

3. Semi-Western Forehand Grip: For many years now the Semi-Western Forehand Grip has been the grip of choice for touring professional players. There is little surprising about this as it gives many specific advantages. Many tennis coaches now promote this grip to their students.

It is best to find the Semi-Western from the Eastern Forehand Grip. All you have to do is rotate your hand a little further clockwise. The base knuckle of your index finger will be on the second bevel while the V of your thumb and forefinger will have moved round to the right side.

+ The big advantage of the Semi-Western Forehand Grip is that it is ideal for big forehand shots from the baseline. It is little wonder, then, that the grip has become such a favorite for professional baseline hitters.

Baseline players adore this grip because it offers such a greater degree of topspin. This allows shots to be played high over the net, while still dipping down within the baseline. You will often see proponents of the Semi-Western making huge swings at the ball, confident the spin will keep the ball in court. For those who enjoy staying further back in the court it is ideal, as it allows the player to take the ball further in front of their body. Another advantage of playing shot with the Semi-Western is that the spin, which drops the ball down quickly, allows the possibility of more angled cross-court shots.

At the same time, the Semi-Western Grip does allow players to hit 'flat' through the ball for a winning passing shot when it is required.

- There are, however, some disadvantages to the Semi-Western Grip. Foremost amongst these is the problem it creates when trying to return low balls. This arises because of the propensity of the Semi-Western to close the face of the racquet. This makes it hard to get the racquet under the ball and lift it over the net. Therefore, while the grip is ideal at the baseline, it is not so useful as the ball gets closer to the net. For those players who enjoy hitting the groundstrokes from the rear of the court, coming to the net presents some problems. Do they try to change their grip or make do?

4. Western Forehand Grip: This may seem like quite an unusual grip at first, maybe even uncomfortable. However, the full Western Forehand Grip has its committed fans. There are mainly those who are proponents of the clay courts and have a game based around building baseline supremacy.

+ The hand position in this grip may seem strange but it has a particular effect. By turning the wrist open before the stroke, the natural movement of the arm means that the wrist is snapped through the ball, bringing the racquet face with it. The overall result is that the strings of the racquet are whipped up and over the ball. This creates a tremendous amount of topspin. Forehand shots played with the Western Grip can be played high over the net and still land in the baseline. The ball will bounce explosively and force your opponent back behind the court.

It is also a great grip for returning those very same high-bouncing balls, especially if the player can get right behind the shot and take the ball early. This makes the grip very useful for younger players.

- As useful as the grip is for high-bouncing balls, it is a real disadvantage when the ball comes hard and fast and low. It can be really difficult, with such a closed face, to adequately return a low ball so that it gets over the net. Moreover, the grip is not much more helpful for volleying and those who use the Western Grip tend to avoid the net.

A further problem affects the ability to play forehand groundstrokes. Because the grip imparts so much topspin, passing shots tend to be less penetrative than those played with a flatter trajectory. The ball loses much of its forward moment when it dips and bounces up. Often players can end up dropping a shot too short because they haven't generated enough pace on the ball.

5. Eastern Backhand Grip: From the forehand grips we are going to move onto examining three backhanded grips. To find these grips we are going to go all the way back to a Continental grip. From this position you are going to turn your hand round counterclockwise (for right-handed players) so that the base knuckle on your forefinger is right on the very top of the handle and the V between forefinger and knuckle is on the fourth bevel.

+ The two biggest advantages of the Eastern Backhand Grip are that it provides good versatility while also allowing a stable position for the wrist. The grip's versatility means that it is possible to play a range of shots adequately. The grip allows players to roll the racquet over the ball to generate topspin. You can also hit straight through the ball in order to maximize power, and it is even possible to hit a backhand slice with the Eastern Grip. It is also a good grip for playing lower balls.

This grip is great for playing what is known as a 'kick serve'. This bounces high and aggressively and is ideal for forcing your opponent play a defensive return.

- Playing an attacking shot with this grip when the ball is low can be difficult. Very often players are forced to slice a passive shot back to their opponent. It is also very difficult to put a lot of topspin on shots, so you may run the risk of either missing the baseline or hitting the net.

6. Extreme Eastern or Semi-Western Backhand Grip: This is a grip that has many advantages but is not the easiest to utilize. Having said that, it is used by some very strong tennis players and is well-worth experimenting with.

You can find the Semi-Western by rotating your whole grip one bevel counterclockwise from Eastern Grip. You should immediately notice that the grip closes the racquet face considerably.

+ Playing with a closed backhand grip has all the advantages of playing with a forehand one. You are able to handle high-bouncing balls much more effectively. Furthermore, you will be able to impart considerable amounts of spin on your shots and control your groundstrokes.

When you use the Semi-Western grip, you will need to hit the ball further through the shot, or before the body and higher up.

- Again, its disadvantages are those we covered when describing the forehand grips. There are problems with trying to return low balls and volleying is a problem. Using this grip tends to mean that players are prepared to spend a lot of time at the baseline and try to dominate their opponent from there.

7. Two-Handed Backhand Grip: It can have escaped tennis fan's notice that in recent decades more and more professional players, both male and female, are using a Two-Handed Backhand Grip.

The backhand grip is certainly effective, however there is much debate about exactly the best way to configure the hands. The usual way is to take the racquet with your right hand (if you are right-handed) in a Continental Grip. Your left hand then grips the handle closer to the racquet head in a Semi-Western Forehand Grip.

+ The main advantage of using this two-handed grip for the backhand is that it adds a tremendous amount of power. This can be extremely useful for the many players who struggle to generate sufficient force on their backhand.

The two-handed player can rely on their shoulder rotation to power the racquet head through the ball. It is a great grip for balls around shoulder height. Many players utilize the two-handed grip to return serve.

- The main disadvantage of a two-handed grip is that it substantially reduces the reach of players. Trying to return any wide shots can prove particularly difficult and players can be vulnerable to them. Even if they can reach the ball, the two-handed player finds it difficult to rotate their shoulders through a ball that is wide. Sometimes players need to use just their arms to get the ball back.

While the two-handed grip offers the possibility of playing shots with a lot of topspin, it is very difficult to play a two-handed shot with any slice. Taking one hand off the racquet every time you want to play a shot with any variety, or that is low or wide, can become problematic. Two-handed players also often have problems volleying or at the net.

Finally, this Youtube video called <u>Tennis Grips</u> by Online Tennis Instruction with Florian Meier demonstrates how to locate the different grips on your racquet.

Chapter 4: Playing Forehand Shots

Any child who picks up a tennis racquet and attempts to hit a ball will, without any encouragement, play a forehand shot. Not only is the forehand the most natural shot to play, it is also the shot that is played more than any other.

Tennis is predominantly a game played with forehand shots. Tennis players require the power and steadiness that a reliable forehand can supply their game.

Establishing a forehand that you can use as the foundation for a great tennis game requires coordinating the following elements:

Start with your stance. The most important element of creating a forehand stroke you can rely on is ensuring that you are playing the shot from a solid base. This means establishing the correct stance that gives you the best foundation to enable you to play your forehand shots with confidence and power.

Stand at the intersection of the baseline and centerline. Feet should be positioned shoulder-width apart. Do not plant your feet squarely down on the court, but keep them relaxed so you can bounce on the balls of your feet. Your knees should be a little bent so that you can feel the flex in the muscles at the front of your thighs, calf muscles and lower back.

This will give you the most stable stance as you swing the racquet from the back behind your right shoulder through, past your waist, up to your left shoulder and finishing around head-height.

Always aim to connect with the sweet spot. The aim of your forehand stroke is to bring the racquet head through the strike zone so that the area in the center of the racquet face connects with the ball. This area of the strings is known as the "sweet spot." The sweet spot gives you the most power and control over the ball, enabling you to play consistent shots that you have control over. Try to feel as if the racquet handle and frame are extensions of your hand and arm. With a little practice, you should begin to feel where the sweet spot is and know when the ball makes contact with it and when it does not.

For a powerful stroke, rotate and extend through the ball. To hit a powerful forehand you need to generate racquet head speed and hit the ball with good timing. There are two ways the body can bring the racquet head through quickly – rotating the arm and extending it.

The most obvious way to play the forehand is to swing the arm from back to front. Our example of a child who has received no coaching will do this naturally. However, you should not only rely on the arm to generate all the power of the shot; the initial movement comes from rotating the core. The hips and the shoulders should turn about ninety degrees in the forehand shot.

Rotating the body involves turning the hips and shoulders back and then releasing them forward, together through the ball. If your feet are planted too firmly onto the court, this will become very awkward. This is why you should stand 'lightly' and your body should be flexed.

Use a pivot to generate extra power. To accommodate and extend the power of the rotation of your hips and shoulders, it is necessary to pivot on the balls of your feet. This prevents your weight from falling over the outside of your knees. Your feet should be at a forty-five degree angle to prevent your weight from tipping over the outside of your ankle.

Extend for added power. The natural way to play the forehand shot is with an outstretched, rotating the shoulder joint such that it looks as if you are waving traffic past. However, more racquet head speed can actually be generated by playing the shot with a flexed arm.

By relaxing the arm, you will find that it naturally folds in as you bring it back to the shoulder. As you strike through the ball and rotate the hips, waist and shoulders, the arm will naturally extend and the elbow and wrist will release, creating much more speed through the strike zone.

Good timing is essential. The key to unleashing this speed effectively is to time your movement so that the foot pivot, hip and shoulder rotation and the arm extension are all coordinated so that they come together as the racquet makes contact with the ball.

Indeed, no matter how much racquet speed you manage to generate, it will all be worthless unless you manage to get the timing of the contact correct. Timing is a very precise skill and will not be mastered overnight.

The perfect height to hit the ball is usually waist-height, or a little higher. Usually, you should be looking to make contact a little in front of the center of the body. This will ensure that the racquet is traveling upwards, the face of the racquet is square and the arm is fully extended. As explained in the previous chapter, different grips will require a slight variation in the strike zone.

Putting it all Together

Playing a great forehand shot is all about putting together the elements outlined above. Of course, this takes practice. In fact, building up a reliable and powerful forehand is divided into two main stages.

Step One: In the first stage, you need to concentrate only on the rotation of the body and the extension of the arm, as outlined above. You should aim to bring all these component parts into one smooth stroke.

To help you concentrate on this, practice hitting your forehand stroke without moving your stance. By keeping your feet in exactly the same position, you reduce the number of movments you need to think about, making it easier to focus on maintaining your balance and a solid base for your stroke.

To be able to practice from the same stance, obviously you need the ball to be fed to the same place every time. This can be done with a playing partner or coach. Using a machine to fire balls with the same velocity and to the same place is ideal.

The are two key points to be aware of when you are putting your forehand stroke together and they are both related to timing. The first point is that the timing of your stroke needs to be coordinated so that each component part unfolds together to bring the racquet through the stroke as smoothly as possible. Aiming for a smooth, natural stroke will ensure that you maximize racquet head speed while minimizing the effort you have to put in.

The second point is that the moment your racquet reaches the maximum speed is also the moment it is facing the target area. This also, of course, needs to coincide with the moment the sweet-spot meets the ball. The ball must meet the sweet spot with the racquet traveling in the direction you wish. You need to be very aware of the point in your stroke that you wish to connect with the ball. For the forehand, this strike-zone is usually a little ahead of center.

Step Two: The second stage of putting together a strong forehand is to add a little movement before finding your stance for the forehand. This progression should only be made when you are confident of your forehand stroke.

First, start with a little lateral movement on the baseline with your coach or training partner hitting balls of the same depth a few meters to either side of the centerline. This will help you to quickly find your balance in the stance, necessary to make a smooth rotation through the stroke. You will find that it is important to get your feet quickly into the right position in order to anticipate the stroke.

Once you become more comfortable with the footwork, you should notice that you will, quite naturally, begin the rotation of the arms and shoulders before you reach the line of the ball. This will enable you to begin the forward stroke as soon as your feet are in the right position.

This video demonstrates how these movements can be put together to create the basic forehand stroke.

More Advanced Techniques

Once you are confident with the basic forehand stroke, you may want to add more advanced techniques to your game.

Progress to the open-shoulder forehand. For extra power, speed and adaptability, many experienced tennis players use an open-shoulder forehand. This differs from the normal forehand in that the rotation of the feet, waist and shoulders is allowed to unwind very much ahead of the arm.

In a normal forehand, when the racquet makes contact with the ball the line across the shoulders will be more or less pointing to where the player wants the ball to go. However, with an open-shoulder forehand, by the time the racquet strikes the ball the shoulders will have progressed through to pointing 45 or even up to 90 degrees (for a right-handed player) to the left of the targe. The opposition player will see the whole of the chest open to them.

The difficulty with this stroke is making sure that the racquet face does not also come through with the shoulders and make the contact with the ball when it is closing.

Add extra topspin for greater power and to enhance your control over the shot. Topspin is a crucial element of any forehand stroke. As we have seen, the grip you use can help here. It is also necessary for the racquet to move through the ball in an upward direction. While the racquet is moving upwards, the racquet face itself will be angled slightly down to enable the strings to run over the ball and impart the spin. By opening the shoulders, as described above, we can create a smoother slide upwards and over the ball.

Generate power and topspin by using your legs. If we want to hit faster, more accurate shots, we have to start from the foundation of our stroke.

To experience how much energy can be generated from the legs alone, you can practice hitting a shot using only the legs. This may sound a little strange, but it is indeed possible. Relax your arms and shoulders and just use the muscles from your waist downwards to rotate around and up through the ball. You will find that, with only these muscles, you can generate quite a bit of power.

Add the power of your shoulders. The legs provide the base and the initial strong movement. The shoulder movement should be added so that it trails a little behind the turning of the hips. The hips initiate the movement and the shoulder rotation reacts and follows through, trying to catch the lower-body.

Whip the arm through the stroke. Like a pitcher in baseball, the unwinding of the body ends in the releasing of the arm. As the shoulders turn, the arm will come behind it and the elbow joint will extend like a whip so that as the racquet comes through the strike zone. At this point, the arm will be nearly straight (though not completely, you should never lock the elbow joint). As the arm goes through the strike zone, you will see how the arm begins to bend, bringing the racquet head upwards.

Through the stroke you will feel your wrist naturally rotate, turning the racquet face. At the point of contact, the wrist will also help to create upward movement and shape the racquet over the ball.

Following this advice should mean that you are playing aggressive but controlled forehand strokes in no time. Check out this video, Forehand Technique – The 5 Power Sources by Daniel Mccain, so see a powerful forehand in action.

Chapter 5: Playing Backhand Shots

Playing the one-handed backhand

For many, the one-handed backhand is the most difficult shot in tennis. Certainly, it has quite a fearsome reputation and many players of all abilities try hard to avoid playing it. It is not unusual to see tennis players "running around" the backhand in order to play a forehand shot instead.

However, with some practice, the backhand can not only save you, but it can also be used as a devastating offensive weapon against your opponents. Believe it or not, it can also become a real pleasure to play and offer real satisfaction in your tennis game.

So avoid the backhand no longer and get ready to learn to love it by following these four steps.

Step One: The fundamentals of the backhand groundstroke are the same as the forehand. Remember to start with a good base with your legs relaxed and knees bent so you can bounce on the balls of your feet.

As with the forehand, the backhand generates power through the rotation of the body that comes first from below the waist and the then the shoulders and arms.

Therefore, at the height of the back swing, your weight will have shifted to be predominantly on your back foot, and your waist will have turned to face the back of the court. However, the difference with the backhand is that your shoulder will be turned to come under your chin. Remember that the racquet should come from a lower position before rising towards the strike zone.

Step Two: Shift the weight from your rear foot towards the front and rotate the waist. Bring the arm around and up towards the strike zone. As with the forehand, the arm will extend as it enters the position at which you intend to hit the ball. Backhands are hit with the leading arm and therefore the strike zone will be level with your leading shoulder.

It is important not to play the ball too close to your body. A common mistake inexperienced players make is to become too constrained in their shot by not giving themselves enough space. The backhand, like the forehand, should be allowed to flow over the ball and this is very difficult to achieve this if the ball is too tight against you. Do not be tempted to wait for the ball to reach your body.

Another major consideration is to always aim to play the ball at around waist-height. Compared to the forehand, the strike zone for the backhand is rather lower and you must be prepared to take the ball when it is closer tot he ground.

Step Three: As you strike the ball, your right arm will have come out so it is level with your shoulder and reaching down to your waist. The arm will be extended, though not locked. Your weight will have shifted from your rear foot to your front foot and your waist will be turning, so it feels as if you are "braced" against your right side.

The power will come from the upward movement made by your leg muscles. You should aim to release this power at the moment of impact.

Your opponent should be able to see your fist facing them as you bring the racquet face square.

Step Four: Despite the power you are trying to generate through the stroke, it is important to remain as balanced as possible. Do not fall away, or spin through the stroke. After contact, keep you weight balanced on you front foot and aim to hold this position as the ball travels over the net. To remain in control of the stroke, try to position your chin over your front foot.

Once these steps are put together you will be able to play a flowing, confident one-handed backhand, as demonstrated in this video by Essential Tennis – Lessons and Instruction for Passionate Players<u>Hit Your Backhand Like Stanislas Wawrinka</u>.

Playing the two-handed backhand

The one-handed backhand can be a dangerous stroke and looks very stylish. However, more and more players are now choosing to play a two-handed backhand instead. There are several good reasons for this shift in technique. First, it can provide more power and control on groundstrokes. Perhaps more importantly, it also enables you to strike the ball when it is higher. This is important when playing against opponents who use a lot of topspin. It also allows players to use it when returning serve.

Step One – The Back Swing

Begin to rotate as soon as possible. Try to spot that you will be playing a backhand as early as possible and begin by turning your body to face the right way. Once you have done this, you can think about rotating your hips and shoulders to prepare for the shot.

Remember to turn from the waist and legs. Don't forget that a good rotation comes from getting the feet and legs in the right position. Turning your shoulders will not be helpful unless you have made sure the foundation of the stroke is in place. You should load your weight onto your rear foot. Once you become more comfortable with your footwork, it will begin to feel as if the shot originates in your legs.

Remember to make a full shoulder turn. Many players using the two-handed backhand go for a big shoulder turn to generate as much power as possible. They may rotate so far as to turn their back to their opponent. That is probably not necessary, but, as with the one-handed back hand, you should have your shoulder under your chin and be looking over it towards the ball.

Arms and wrists should also prepare for the stroke. The legs and core start the rotation but the arms and wrists are used to give that full extension on the backswing. Your elbow and wrist joints should lift upwards until the racquet is at waist height and facing away from the net. It is by extending the turn in this way that you generate more power in the shot. Remember that to add topspin to the shot, we need to be moving over the ball by swinging from low to high with your arms.

Step Two – Through the Strike Zone

Stay relaxed as you strike the ball. As you rotate through the strikezone, the key is to remain as relaxed as possible. Any tension in the shoulders or arms will only result in the shot becoming awkward. We don't want to force the ball with our arms; instead we want to make the stroke as smooth as possible.

Take the time to practice with your weaker hand. The two-handed backhand gets its extra element of control and power by allowing your weaker hand to help out. To further develop your weaker hand and make it even more useful, you might want to practice a little by using it alone. This will help you feel the shot a lot more through your weaker arm.

Use the power from your legs and torso and transfer it through the racquet to the ball. Because the two-handed backhand allows the additional strength of your weaker arm to help out, many players forget the importance of rotating through the shot with their body. The legs and waist are just as important when you use two hands as when you use one.

Always ensure that you've got your footwork right. To ensure you rotate correctly, check that you are shifting the weight from your rear foot to front foot. When you are coming through the strike zone, your weight should be moving your weight onto your front foot. Remember to maintain your balance. Keep on the balls of your feet and don't "step-through" the shot.

Step Three – The Follow-Through

Remember to continue to rotate your body in the follow-through. If you have got the rotation right, you will rotate through the stroke so that your follow-through takes you back to facing the net. This is ideal because it shows you have released all the energy in the rotation, and it brings you back ready for the next shot. Be careful not to fall through the shot or lose your balance. You can avoid this by remaining on the balls of your feet and keeping your stance light.

Once you master the two-handed backhand you are on the way to becoming a very modern and adept tennis player. Check your technique against the demonstration in this YouTube video by Top Tennis Training: Hit Your Backhand Like Djokovic.

Playing the backhand slice

Up til now we have been talking about shots that impart some degree of topspin on the ball, by rolling the racquet up over the ball. Slice is essentially the opposite. The strings are run down the ball, creating backspin that produces shots with a much lower trajectory. Sliced shots stay very flat and their bounce is low. This can make them a very useful weapon and good addition to your game. The slice is best played with a backhand stroke.

The backhand slice can be used as a way to help you approach the net. Many professional players use the backhand as a precursor to approaching the net. The low bounce means that their opponents are forced to hit their returns slightly higher, giving the onrushing player an easier volley once he reaches the net..

The slice can be used as an effective defensive measure. Players such as Serena Williams often use the backhand slice as a defensive measure, when the ball is out to the side of the court as a sliced backhand is a good shot to play when you are stretched. The low bounce will help prevent the opponent from playing a winning shot.

Step One – The Back Swing

Before starting, check you've got your grip right. Shifting from topspin to backspin requires us to check on our grip. In order to play the backhand slice, you will need to use the Continental grip, as outlined above.

As your prepare for the stroke, adopt the 'ready' body position. As you wait for the ball, your weaker hand should be just touching the racquet at the base of the frame. This is a good position from which to react to whatever shot comes your way and remain flexible enough to play from a range of shots yourself.

Turn your feet, waist and shoulders. As with the one and two-handed backhand strokes, once you realize you will be playing a backhand shot, you need to first turn your feet and waist and begin to rotate your shoulders so that your right shoulder is pointing to the ball.

The arm movement distinguishes the slice from the topspin. The difference between the slice and the topspin becomes apparent as you move your arms back. To hit a slice, the shoulders turn to bring the racquet back to a 'high' position, even with your head. To help you do this, you may wish to leave your non-hitting hand on the racquet frame as an additional guide to get it in the right position.

Step Two – Through the Strike Zone

The weight is shifted from the back foot to the front. When you are preparing for this stroke you should begin to load your weight onto your back foot. As you rotate and pivot, your weight is released forwards. However, unlike the topspin stroke, the legs are not pushing upwards through the stroke. Instead, you should shifting the weight forward and down. As the racquet moves through the strike zone, you should lean into the shot, feeling the weight go down through the front-foot.

Impart spin onto the tennis ball with a downward, slicing action. The purpose of this downward action is to slice through the ball, spinning it backwards. The movement of the racquet will feel like a knife, slicing from high to low. The strings will feel as if they are grating against the ball. If played correctly, the effect will be obvious as the ball "fizzes" off the racquet.

Step Three – The Follow-Through

Extend the follow-through towards your target. After contact, continue your stroke by fully extending the forearm until it is out in front of the body. Try to continue looking at the strike zone for a second or two after contact as been made. This will ensure you maintain a good position through the stroke. As you extend, remember to continue the high-to-low shape and slice downwards.

Use your non-racquet hand to balance. This slicing down motion may be a little difficult to control at first. To ensure that you keep your balance, you may want to extend your other hand upwards and behind you to act as a counter-balance to your forward stroke.

The backhand slice is a lovely shot to play and to master. Here it is demonstrated on this YouTube video: How to Hit a Tennis Slice Backhand by Top Speed Tennis.

Chapter 6: The Serve

Start with the Right Grip

There are two grips that are most often used for the serve: Continental and the Eastern Forehand grip. Many players begin learning to serve by first adopting the Eastern Forehand grip. This grip can feel more comfortable and may be the most straightforward technique to begin serving in a way that can reliably clear the net and get into the service box.

However, this grip tends to result in a serve with a "flat" shape. This can be problematic as this gives the server little clearance room over the net. For the serve, the Eastern Forehand grip can be thought of as a way to start, a beginners grip.

In comparison, the Continental grip results in serves with a lot more topspin. It is also useful because it encourages players to fully extend the arm through the serve and creates a better angle of shot. For these reasons, unless you find it just too uncomfortable, many coaches recommend starting with the Continental grip.

Let your natural action impart spin on the ball. The advantage of the Continental grip will soon be apparent. Once you are able to serve adequately, you will find that you naturally impart a fair amount of both topspin and sidespin on the ball. The advantages of this, in terms controlling the ball, will be very clear and enough to encourage you to persist with the Continental grip.

Start by getting your stance right. This is particularly important for the serve as it is the only shot in which you can position yourself. As such, there is no excuse for not getting your stance right. Start by pointing your front foot towards the right-hand net post (for right-handed players). The rear foot should be turned so it is parallel to the baseline.

To wind-up, or not to wind-up. We have all seen professional players with their big wind-ups before they serve. Like the big rotation in the back swing of the groundstrokes, the wind-up is used to generate more power through the serve. However, this is not absolutely necessary to learn to serve, nor to serve adequately.

In the step-by-step guide that follows, the "wind-up" is the full bending of the elbow and the bending of the knees to prepare for a big spring upwards.

The crucial point is not to become too fixated on the wind-up when there are more important aspects of the serve that you need to ensure you master first. The wind-up will not help you generate any effective power if you are not bending your elbow correctly, or making contact with the ball when it is high. Once you have these in place, it is not too difficult to begin to increase your wind-up.

Mastering a reliable toss is crucial for an effective serve. You will never serve well unless you can put the ball in the right place. The toss is a vital but often overlooked element of the serve.

What you are aiming to achieve with a toss is to be able to throw the ball up to the same point each time. To do this you should avoid throwing the ball up in any sort of a curve. Rather, you should attempt to make the ball go up and down in a straight line. This simplicity will allow you to repeat the same toss again and again.

Start by holding the ball lightly with your fingertips. Let your arm hang down naturally, so that it is relaxed. As this will be your leading arm, you are likely to be holding it down from your shoulder, a little way in front of your head and a little way out of your body.

You are then going to imagine a line that goes straight up from the ball. You need to bring your arm up so that the ball slides up this line. Keep your grip on the ball relaxed so that when you release, the ball continues to travel up this vertical line. This does take practice because simply raising an extended arm actually creates a curve and will cause you to throw a ball that is going to come up towards you.

At first, you may have a tendency to throw the ball so that it goes up and down in a curve. If this happens, simply catch the ball and try again. Don't be tempted to practice your serve on a bad toss; it won't be beneficial. This discipline is also useful for in a game. Going through with the serve when you know the toss is not good enough is unlikely to result in a good serve.

Step One – The Toss and Back Swing

Tilt your shoulders. Once you start to bring the tossing arm upward, you will also feel the shoulder rise so that it comes up under your chin as you follow the ball with your eyes. Your other shoulder will drop down.

Before you release the ball, your hitting arm will swing backwards. The racquet arm will also drop down. This arm should be bent about ninety degrees at the elbow, with the racquet head coming back behind the head. As this happens you will also feel your weight shift back onto your rear foot.

Remember to bend the both the elbow and wrist. It's worth repeating: To generate any power and spin on the serve (which is crucial if you want to serve effectively), you must bend your elbow on the back swing. Once you reach the full extent of your back swing, the racquet head should be hanging down behind your head. This can only be achieved if your elbow is bent and your wrist is relaxed and 'cocked' back. Not only does this guarantee you get extra power but it also reduces the likelihood of injuries.

Release the ball when your arm is high. Aim to extend your arm as high as possible while still maintaining control and the straight, vertical line discussed in the previous step. Again, always try to release the ball with relaxed fingers, as this will prevent the ball from going off course. To ensure an accurate toss, imagine spreading your fingers all at once, like the opening of the petals of a flower, and try to continue the upward movement of your wrist along the same line for a few centimeters after you have released the ball.

Step Two – The Store

Prepare for the spring by bending your knees. Another common mistake made when players are attempting to improve their serve is to bend their legs too early. The legs must only be bent after the upward motion of the toss is complete. Trying to simultaneously bend down and reach up will only be counterproductive.

Instead, the bend should come very swiftly after the ball has been released and be a very rapid and short accumulation of the shift of your weight to the rear foot.

Think of your body as a coiled spring. Once you have released the ball at the top of the toss, you should bend both knees. This step is called the Store because it is at this point that you are storing the maximum amount of potential energy before releasing it into the serve.

Your arm will be back in a horizontal position with both your elbow bent and your wrist cocked. Your weight will be shifted back onto your rear foot, acting much like a pivot. In the same way, the shoulder of your hitting arm will have dropped below the other. Your legs will be bent, compressing all the energy in your body low down and to your right. This energy will be released through the serve.

Step Three – The Spring

Initiate the spring from the feet. Although the energy is built up slowly, the bending of the knees is the last stage, and, once they bend, this is the signal for the spring to begin.

The trigger for the spring comes from right down in the feet as they switch from being compressed to springing back upwards.

Release the energy through your body as you spring upwards. As in the groundstrokes, the latent energy contained in the back swing is released through a chain of movements. It starts in the balls of the feet and moves up through the lower legs to the knees, which begin to straighten. The energy then moves up through your waist and core to pivot through your shoulders, sending the hitting arm upwards.

Keep your elbow up and your racquet-head down until the last moment. In truth, although it is interesting to think about this chain of movements, you will most likely follow this sequence quite naturally. One thing worth bearing in mind is the need to keep your elbow bent and your wrist cocked. Do this by not hurrying into the shot and keeping your arm relaxed. This way your arm will bring the racquet head through the ball at just the right time with the maximum speed.

Step Four – Bringing The Racquet Through The Strike Zone

Straighten your elbow and wrist. Once the legs straighten and the energy transfers up through the body, the shoulder of your hitting arm should be raised and the elbow nice and high. At this point the arm will also straighten through the elbow joint.

The very last part of your body to straighten is your wrist. Up to the last moment before contact the wrist is cocked back about 90 degrees. Finally, all the energy of the serve is released through the wrist, sending the racquet quickly through the strike zone in a whipping motion.

Let your wrist come forward naturally. The movement outlined above is responsible for sending your racquet at high-speed. However, do not be tempted to force the racquet through the strike zone with either your elbow or wrist. Some players try to "snap" their wrist to gain extra power. This is not necessary, and, in fact, it may damage your arm. In the long-run, forcing wrist movement and will only prove counterproductive.

By keeping your elbow and wrist relaxed, you allow the serve to be controlled by the major muscles, which increases its reliability. The elbow and wrist will automatically whip through the ball without you trying to force it, and the wrist cock will naturally be released as your larger muscles bring the racquet through the strike zone. By keeping the wrist relaxed and letting it unfurl naturally through the shot, you will transfer all your energy into the ball.

Let the racquet-edge lead cut through the stroke and let the face open naturally. As the racquet is brought up from behind the head to the strike zone it will be held edge-first. However, as the elbow and wrist straighten, the racquet face will open to allow the strings to face the ball. As long as your arm is kept relaxed, your grip will ensure the racquet is brought around to the correct position.

Just before contact you should assume the correct stance. As your racquet-head comes into the strike zone, you will shift all of your weight upwards and to your leading leg. The spring should be so profound that it will almost (or actually does) bring your rear foot off the court.

From a side on stance, when you began your toss, your shoulders will have pivoted so that your hitting shoulder has come round to face the front and your whole body is now facing the net.

Step Five - Contact

Always strive to connect with the ball at exactly the right point. Although this may seem like an obvious and straightforward tip, it is not always so simple as it sounds. If we return to the toss, you will recall that we are attempting to take the ball up in a straight line that is both a little in front of the head and away from the body. Although the perfect point to strike the ball will vary a little from player to player, most coaches agree that a foot in front of your head and about a foot to the right is ideal.

The ideal point will be where it does not feel as if you have to reach for the ball, nor where it feels as if the serve is crowding your body.

Hit the ball at the apex of the toss. The next question is how high on its vertical path you should meet the ball. The easy answer is as high as possible. A common problem is not extending fully through the serve and hitting the ball too low. Going through the serve very slowly and observing exactly where your racquet passes with a full extension of the arm, shoulder and the right foot raising off the ground rectify this. Once you have established this, you should work on your toss to make sure that the ball is at least this high.

Step Six – The Follow-Through

As with the groundstrokes, a good tip is to keep watching your racquet until it completes its arc through strike zone, even after you have struck the ball. This ensures that you maintain good form as you strike the ball.

Follow through with the racquet pulling down your left side. A powerful serve will send the racquet all the way through the strike zone and down the other side. It may seem that it will finish by hitting your legs, but it will pass down your left side. The forward motion generated by your serve pushes your rear foot forward and you may step over the baseline.

The serve is an absolutely crucial element of any tennis game and one that many players struggle with. This YouTube video by Tennis Now shows how players such as Serena Williams keep their serves simple to ensure consistency: How to Hit a Serve – Taking a Lesson from Serena Williams.

Chapter 7: Hitting a Volley

Hitting the ball before it has bounced, or "volleying," is a shot that every tennis player needs in their arsenal. Volleying requires a special technique. Once the ball has hit the court it loses up to half its velocity. As a result it is much more difficult to control a volley.

However, the volley is an excellent shot to be able to use in a match. By taking a shot early, before it has bounced, you are effectively reducing your opponent's reaction time. Volleys are often responsible for winning the point.

Here are 7 steps that will help you execute a precise and devastating volley.

Step One - See the ball early and watch it hit the racquet

If you are intending to play a volley you will not have anything like the time to prepare that you have playing from the back of the court. To deal with this, you need to watch the ball from the moment it leaves your opponent's racquet until it makes contact with yours.

This concentration on the ball is a vital and often overlooked element of volleying. Yet, anyone who watches professional players when they come in to volley can't help but notice the tremendous focus they have on the ball. By watching the ball carefully, they are not only looking out for the direction and speed of the ball, but also noticing how the ball is spinning.

Step Two – Think about your positioning

When you are volleying you have a lot less time to prepare for the shot, as a result it is vital that you get your positioning right.

Volleying requires that you get close to the net. Avoid getting caught in what is known as 'no-man's land' – the area between baseline and service line. Here you will find yourself either having to hi-low volleys, or take the ball on the half-volley. Instead, you should be well inside the service line. This gives you the added advantage of narrowing the angle and preventing reaching the ball before it passes you. It also improves the angle at which you can play a volley into the opponent's court and increases your chance of playing a winning shot.

Step Three – Bounce and stay mobile

It is vital to remain mobile and flexible in order to quickly change direction and get in the right position to volley correctly. To "bounce" refers to the need to stay on the balls of your feet, constantly bouncing. This will help you react as rapidly as possible and alter your position and stance to play your next shot. In order to bounce, your legs need to be flexed and bent at the knees. The worst thing you can do is to plant your feet too squarely in the ground; this will only result in you being unable to react quickly enough.

Always bend your knees. This allows you to reach down to low volleys or jump to get higher balls.

Step Four – Move forward towards the ball

Volleying is an aggressive shot. The idea is to drive the ball back into the opponent's court before they have a chance to react. However, a large back swing is not necessary.; the racquet is simply used to redirect the energy of your opponents shot. Control is the primary concern. A short smooth back swing, controlled by your shoulder, and the forward motion of your body is enough.

You should be watching the ball until it hits the racquet, but you should also be moving towards the ball to meet it. Controlling volleys is a lot easier if you meet the ball before it has reached your body. It is very difficult to control a volley if the ball has begun to go past you.

You should also seek to reach your volley when the ball is still above the height of the net. This will give you the best opportunity to control a winning shot. Furthermore, it will enable you to reapply all the velocity back onto the ball without having to worry about "cushioning" the volley in order to get it up and down again.

Step Five - Turn to volley

Much like groundstrokes, volleys should be hit side-on to the ball. Make an early decision about which side you want to hit the ball from. This might be a split second decision as the ball will come at your very quickly, but it is important not to take the ball square on, so be prepared to move rapidly to one side.

Your leading shoulder should be pointed towards the ball. Bend your elbow slightly to position the racquet head at the same height as your shoulder. For lower balls, your knees need to be bent and you must get your shoulder down to the height of the ball.

Contact should be made when your racquet is level with your shoulder. This will give you the best control over the shot.

Step Six – The Follow-Through

In the same way that there is no real back swing on your volleys, it is also not necessary to have an extravagant follow-through. Instead, you should imagine pushing the racquet head smoothly through the ball. The racquet should not cut across the strike zone, but only follow the line of the shot.

They key to successful volleying is to get in position early, get side on, and take the ball as high as possible. Start by establishing a nice shape with your leading shoulder and ensure the racquet head is correctly aligned. The best players of the volley always watch the ball all the way onto their strings. If you can do this, your volleying will be very effective. Simplicity is the key here. From close range, with modern equipment, you can rely on your solid technique to win you the point. This video, Tennis Volley Technique by Top Tennis Training, demonstrates a great volleying technique.

Chapter 8: Playing Doubles

Although there are a number of differences in the rules and in playing singles and doubles, the game really differs in terms of the strategy and psychology that come into play. For this reason, many players find doubles a very rewarding form of the sport. Many people also claim that playing doubles can be very effective in developing areas of your singles game. If you do not already, playing doubles is certainly something you should consider. With a little attention to the particular tactics and techniques required, you can significantly improve your doubles game.

The basic differences between singles and doubles

Once you are familiar with the basic regulations of doubles, governing the use of the sidelines, the order of serve, you should begin to consider how you are going to divide the court between you and your partner. Apart from when you receive the serve and when you keep the same side of the court through the match, how you divide the court is entirely between you and your partner.

Dividing the game between you and your partner

Each partner should work a side of the court they are happy with. The side from which you return serve will always be the same, so it makes sense to organize with your partner so that you are both at your stronger side. If you have one right-hander and one left-hander, it is a no-brainer. If not, you will need to settle on system that best utilizes a backhand return.

Organize the order of serving. You will need to consider which of you has the most effective serve and when this should best be used. Should it be put up straight away, to try to dominate the set from the off, or would it be better to keep a powerful service game in reserve?

Mastering the doubles game requires an understanding of shot-selection, court positioning and strategy.

This is not the only element of serving that needs to be considered. When one player is serving, the other needs to know what kind of serve to expect in order to prepare himself or herself for your opponent's return. Doubles partners often have a way of communicating the nature of the serve to come to maximize this advantage. In general terms, there needs to be an agreement on where exactly the non-serving player should stand. This will depend on the overall strategy you are looking to implement in the match.

Look to serve down the middle. As in singles, the serving and returning are where the majority of points are won and lost in doubles. A powerful and accurate serve is always an effective weapon. In singles it is often used to move a player wide of the court. In contrast, a more common technique in doubles is to serve straight and fast down the centerline.

Use the serve to set up a winning volley. Serving down the middle may limit your ability to serve an ace. Instead, the serve is used as a precursor to your partner taking control of the net. By serving down the middle, you have reduced your opponent's angles and allowed your partner to move to the net to look for a winning volley.

Always think carefully about your return. In singles you may wish to hit your returns either down the line or cross-court. However, in doubles the option of playing down the line is not so attractive as it offers the possibility of your opponent moving across the net and having an angle to play a cross-court volley.

Playing your return cross-court is the safer option. The classic doubles return is cross-court played with a lot of topspin so that your opponent has to dig out a volley from near their toes. They will be forced to play an upwards volley from the center of the court with no angle to attack you.

A basic strategy is to stay in the point longer than your opponents. In doubles the reduction of space in the court puts a premium on you and your partner's ability to remain in the point as long as possible. For beginners, the best strategy might simply be continue the point as long as possible and increase the pressure on your opponents until they make a mistake. As doubles players become more experienced, their strategy is likely to develop.

Special shot selection for doubles

The particular differences between singles and doubles put a greater emphasis on some specific shots.

Always try to work on the angles for shots. A key idea for doubles is to always try to work on producing angles and spaces between your opponents. The presence of two players puts an emphasis on being able to control a rally in order to pull players out of position.

Recognize the importance of controlling the net. The ability to control the net is highly prized in doubles. Not only is moving to the net less risky, because you can position one player to patrol the baseline, but points are also very often won at the net because it opens up a range of angles to exploit. You can also be in the best position to play shots between your opponents.

Be prepared to move both players up to the net. The most common strategy is to have one player attacking at the net, while the other is in a more defensive position patrolling the baseline. However, a pair can look to dominate the court by moving both players up to the net, making it very difficult for their opponents to play past them. This highlights the importance of having a solid technique for volleying in a game of doubles.

Learn how to volley effectively in order to dominate doubles. In singles, a volley is very often the point-ending stroke. In doubles, however, there can often be rallies featuring a number of volleys.

Be prepared to counteract the lob. With all the volleying at the net, doubles matches very often feature players trying the aerial route to counteract opponents positioned at the net. There are two ways to deal with the lob. The first is to be quick over the ground to retrieve it. The second is to put high balls away with overhead shots.

Make use of the overhead shot to win points. The overhead shot is crucial in doubles. If a team has a good overhead shot, it can be very difficult for opponents to play against them, as any loose, high ball is an invitation to hit a winner. There is a slight strategic difference when playing an overhead in doubles compared to singles. Rather than look to create angles and play the overhead wide of your opponent, it is better to hit the overhead down the center of the court between your opponents.

Make sure you put away those overheads. Whenever you get an opportunity for an overhead smash, be sure not to waste it. Use a similar technique to your serve. Your non-hitting hand will "spot" the ball onto the racquet, as it does in the toss of the serve. Always be sure you have a stable base and play the shot in a controlled way – it is not necessary to strike the ball very hard. Instead, use the technique, practiced in the service to ensure that the racquet head comes through the strike zone accurately.

Look to exploit the space down the middle of the court. As with the return of serve, groundstrokes are often best played down what is known as the "alley" the gap between your two opponents.

Try to keep passing shots low over the net. When you are playing against a partnership that is looking to dominate the net and attack, be careful with the passing shots you play. In singles it is acceptable to hit shots to the baseline that loop high over the net. However, in doubles, these are liable to be intercepted by a volley. A high ball is relatively easy to volley and put away for a win.

In this case, it is far better to hit flatter shots that do not have so much air. A sliced backhand is an ideal choice foe this as it stays very low.

As with almost all elements of doubles, how effectively you play these shots depends on how well you and your partner work together.

Be prepared for the psychology of doubles

Playing doubles always adds an extra element of psychology. The extra, maybe intangible, element of doubles is always, of course, the other player.

Choose your doubles partner carefully. The first stage of developing teamwork with your partner is choosing them. When professional players pick their doubles partners, they do so very carefully. They must consider the technical aspect – how their game compliments their partners and vice versa. Another important aspect is their approach to the match and their views on overall tennis strategy. If there is no agreement here, the partnership will always be a difficult one. Potential partners must also pay particular attention to how well their personalities will work together. Throughout tennis matches, doubles partners are continually engaged in spoken and non-verbal communication. The partnership cannot be successful if this communication does not work well.

Working with another tennis player is a lot different to simply working against one. Do not underestimate the psychological component of doubles. It is a team sport, but one that is very condensed and intense, which puts great strain on the partnership.

Tennis players have to be mentally tough, and the mental strength of a good partnership can be exponentially more than its component parts. Alternatively, a partnership that sours can result in collapsing teamwork, trust and camaraderie.

Be ready to deal with errors. When things are going well on the court, doubles is a joy to play. One player's confidence can rub off on the other, and congratulating your partner on a great shot can almost feel as good as being congratulated yourself.

However, it is not always like this. All tennis players make errors. Often they are unforced, and bad tennis shots can look very bad indeed. In singles, this is a problem and you have to rely on your own mental strength to cope with it and turn your form around. Dealing with this in doubles is a whole different struggle.

Making a mistake that also lets your partner down can make many people feel self-conscious and worse than if it only affected them. Perhaps an even bigger issue is how to react to mistakes your partner makes.

Always stay positive. This might seem an oversimplification, but there really is no other choice. Whatever the situation, or however bad the error, there is nothing to be gained by being too hard on yourself or angry with your partner. In tennis, when the point is lost, it is gone. Unless it is match point, you just have to fight for the next one. Leave any analysis of your game until after the match, clear your mind and collectively move on.

Good communication is the best way to avoid creating a conflict with your partner. This communication should include agreeing on a clear and workable game plan prior to the match, encouraging each other throughout the match and honestly evaluating your game once it is complete.

And finally, do not go easy on your opponents. They are unlikely to go easy on you, so do not hesitate to exploit the weaknesses apparent in your opponent's team. If there is one player who is struggling, you can target them.

Chapter 9: Exercises and Training Strategies

No matter what level you compete at, you will be able to benefit from some off-season strategies. The first thing that you should do is get enough sleep every day. When you are playing competitively, your sleep schedule is going to get all messed up with the planes, buses, cars, and hotel stays. Figure out a way to get on a more consistent sleep schedule to let your body some rest before the season starts again. Aim for 8 hours or more of sleep each night.

Keep your diet clean. Even in the off-season you should avoid processed and fast food. These might taste good, but they are going to be hard on your body and you don't want to get your butt kicked when you go back for training.

Next, concentrate on hydration. When you are not out in the sun or running around, it is easy to forget that you are thirsty and need to watch your fluid intake. Take the time to drink plenty of water because your muscles will still need the hydration to be strong once the season starts again.

During the off-season, take care of the past injuries you may have suffered. These might be slowing down your game and it will be easier to get injured again if you don't strengthen them again properly. Go through a thorough assessment with a doctor or a athletic trainer to see where injuries might be present, especially if you have been injured recently. They can help you to get on the path to healing the injury and preventing another from occurring.

Laying a new foundation and preparing for the next season is important for your off-season training. You cannot afford to take the whole off-season "off" if you want to be better than the rest. You should have some sort of training program in place during the off-season that will help you to get the edge that you want and to perform your very best when the season begins again.

Best Workouts for Training

To be on your game all of the time, you need to make sure that you are getting the right workouts in. While running can help you out, some extra work targeting specific muscles will do wonders for your game. Whether you want to be even better during the season or if you just make sure that you do not get behind in the off-season, these 10 exercises can help you to get in the best shape for playing tennis.

1. **Squats**- Squats are one of the best workouts for building up your upper leg muscles. To do this, begin by standing with your feet about shoulder width apart. Keep the spine straight while sticking the butt out and lowering the body so the knees make a 90-degree angle. Slowly straighten your legs until you are back to the starting position. Do at least 10 reps for each set and aim for at least 3 sets to

get the best results. Here is a great YouTube video on How to do a Squat by Howcast.

2. **Sprints**- Sprints are a great exercise to do in order to get in cardio as well as to build up your speed. You should only need to complete this exercise 2 times a week in order to increase the muscle mass of your legs. To start, go to a track and go as fast as you can for 50 feet, then jog for an additional 50 feet, then repeat. Over time, you will be able to increase the length of time you are able to sprint for maximum results. Check out this great YouTube video by DeStorm Power called: How to Sprint- Pt. 1

3. **Uphill runs**- This adds another level to sprinting that targets some new muscles in the legs. If you are able to do this effectively, you will be amazed at how much stronger and faster you will be. To do this, you need to go out and find a nice sized hill. Start out small and then can build up to larger hills as you get stronger. Start at the bottom of the hill and sprint up as fast as possible. After you reach the top, lightly jog back down to the bottom of the hill. Do this at least 5 times. For some more tips on uphill runs, check out this YouTube video called Uphill Running Techniques and Cues by James Dunne.

4. **Power Jumps**- When you do a powerful jump, you challenge your leg muscles in new ways.. You can work all parts of the leg with these jumps. The key to doing them is to go quickly and to get as much power and height as you can. To start, stand with your feet about shoulder width apart. Get into a half-squat and then use all of your might to jump as high as possible. Do at least 20 reps of these per set and as many sets as you can. For a visual example of how to do this check out this YouTube video called Power Jumps by Danielle Hinson.

5. **Lateral Bounds**- To do these, begin by putting your weight on the right leg. Load onto the leg by sitting into the hips and bending your knee. Jump laterally as far and high as you can before landing on the other leg. Swing your arms in order to get some more power. Pause for 3 seconds in between bounds and then slowly go faster over time. Check out this YouTube video called: Exercise Tutorial-- Lateral Bound by CompoundConditioning for a demonstration.

6. **Explosive push-ups**- Start in the down position for a pushup. Push upwards explosively letting your hands leave the floor. Try to land softly and have the elbows bent and your core tight. Then lower the chest to the floor before doing another explosive push up. To see this in action check out this YouTube video called Exercise of the Week: Explosive Push Ups by Maximized Living.

7. **Split jumps**- Jumping can do so much to help the muscles in the leg and this exercise will give you the muscles you are looking for. To start this workout, stand with the right foot out in front in a staggered position. Bend your knees so you are doing a lunge, keeping the core tight and the chest up. Jump up as high as you can, and while in the air, scissor kick the legs so that the left foot is in the front.

Do this back and forth. To see this in action check out this YouTube video called How to perform a Split Jump by Iron Core Kettlebells.

8. **T-Hop drill-** Begin by making a 2-foot by 2-foot "T" on the ground using some tape. With your feet together, start hopping backward and forward going as fast as you can. Progress on to have 2 foot hops and going in different directions. Slowly progress to hopping on one foot.

9. **Circuit training-** If you are at a gym to do a workout, take the time to check out circuit training areas or at least go back and forth between different machines and make up your own. This allows you to work on multiple parts of your body, including weight training and cardio, to get the best workout possible. Check out this YouTube video called: Functional Tennis - Interval circuit training for tennis players by Functional Tennis for some great circuit training ideas.

10. **Hitting drills-** Of course, if you want to have the muscles for hitting the ball, you need to practice. Go against a wall and practice the different strokes that need to be done. You can do a few that are soft, a few from the side, and some that are really hard. Mix it up in order to get the best results in the least amount of time. Check out this video by expertvillage on YouTube on How to Correctly Hit a Tennis Ball to get more ideas on working those hitting muscles.

11. **Leg Extensions, Hamstring Curls & Calf Raises-** These three exercises should be a basic staple of all tennis players. Be sure to include them in your regular exercise routine to make sure you are keeping your entire legs strong. Hamstring curls are especially important as many people tend to over train their quads, which can lead to hamstring injuries later on. Calf muscles can be trained every day.

You can choose which exercises you would like to do in order to get the best workout, but these will help to get you started in the right direction. Be sure to include your favorite exercises in your routine and find out just how much stronger and faster you can become.

Avoiding Injury from Overtraining

If you want to see some great results at the gym and in your workouts, you need to make sure that you are not overtraining. This has been the downfall of many great athletes! You may feel motivated and excited to see great results, but when you overdo it in the workouts, you will find that it is going to make you inefficient in your matches because your muscles are tired and not getting the rest that they need. In addition, you are more likely that you will be injured in the process. You will be much better off in the long run to eat healthy, stretch, relax and employing strategies like visualization instead of pushing your body too hard. Here are some great ways to reduce the chances of overtraining while still getting in some amazing workouts that will put you ahead of the game. Check out this great

YouTube video called: <u>Overtraining-How Much Training is Too Much?</u> by VergieConditioning's channel for more information on overtraining.

Here are some helpful recovery tips:

1. **Reduce time at the gym-** When you are trying to build up muscle, more is not always better. You need to give your muscles some time to recover between workouts so that they have the chance to grow. You should never go to the gym more than 5 days each week, and depending on how hard you work out, 3 days may be fine. 45 to 60 minutes is long enough to be at the gym to get results. If you feel like you should go more often, switch up days and do one of muscle building and one of cardio so your muscles still get a break. It's always a good idea to do strength training before cardio training for the best results.

2. **Give your muscles a break-** Always rest your muscles after a workout in order to make sure that they have time to heal. An average person will need a week between working out each muscle group to fully recover, but as an athlete who is conditioned, you probably do not need that long. However, you will still need to give the muscle groups several days to recover before working them out again.

3. **Get some rest-** Your muscles are never going to be able to recover properly if you are not getting the sleep that you need in order to look and feel your very best. Make sure that you are getting at least 8 hours of sleep a night in order to recharge, especially during the season since you will be working hard.

4. **Get enough to eat-** The more that you workout, the more you will need to eat of the right kinds of foods, to get the nutrients that your needs in order to grow the muscles. Nutrients are also important in helping the muscles recover. Eat foods that are high in nutrients for the best results and avoid foods with lots of sugars and other bad things in them.

5. **Take a shower-** Yes, taking a shower can help you to not only smell good after a workout, but it is also good for helping your muscles to recover. When in the shower, start with the water on as hot as you can take it for a minute and then you can switch to the coldest that you can take it for an additional minute, making sure to keep it on the muscles that were worked out. Do this 3 to 4 times for the best results.

6. **Ice Packs & Electrical Stimulation-** Ice packs and electrical stimulation can help with injuries and help prevent an injury from getting worse. A few reusable <u>ice packs</u> and a <u>tens electrical machine</u> are great investments and should be used as often as necessary.

Conclusion

Playing your very best in tennis is going to take some time and effort and you will not be able to do it by being lazy and hoping that the best will happen. You have to be dedicated to the game and give it your all each and every practice in order to be the best and blow away the competition.

By utilizing the strategies in this book along with some dedication and hard work you should be able to see some incredible results. Take the top five strategies or tips that you have just discovered and begin to apply them immediately! Continue doing them until they have been mastered, then choose another five strategies to work on. Be sure that you are reviewing your tennis goals daily and that you are keeping yourself in positive frame of mind. Remember that tennis is a team game, so just play your best and trust your teammates. Be sure to share your knowledge with your friends and teammates so they can get better as well. By focusing your attention on the most important skills and strategies that will improve your game the most, it won't be too long before you are one of the best players around and someone your coaches and teammates will greatly admire!

Finally, if you discovered at least one thing that has helped you or that you think would be beneficial to someone else, be sure to take a few seconds to easily post a quick positive review. As an author, your positive feedback is desperately needed. Your highly valuable five star reviews are like a river of golden joy flowing through a sunny forest of mighty trees and beautiful flowers! *To do your good deed in making the world a better place by helping others with your valuable insight, just leave a nice review.*

My Other Books and Audio Books
www.AcesEbooks.com

Popular Books

BASEBALL
BASEBALL STRATEGIES

THE TOP 100 BEST WAYS TO IMPROVE YOUR BASEBALL GAME

ACE McCLOUD

GOLF
GOLF STRATEGIES

The Perfect Swing
Golf Game Preparation

Ace McCloud

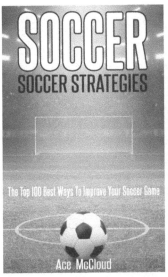

SOCCER
SOCCER STRATEGIES

The Top 100 Best Ways To Improve Your Soccer Game

Ace McCloud

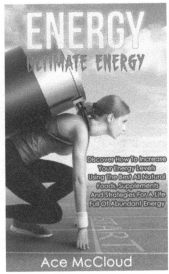

ENERGY
ULTIMATE ENERGY

Discover How To Increase Your Energy Levels Using The Best All Natural Foods, Supplements And Strategies For A Life Full Of Abundant Energy

Ace McCloud

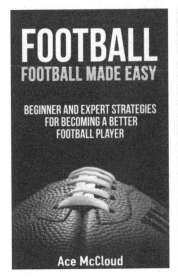

FOOTBALL
FOOTBALL MADE EASY

BEGINNER AND EXPERT STRATEGIES FOR BECOMING A BETTER FOOTBALL PLAYER

Ace McCloud

MOTIVATION

MASTER THE POWER OF MOTIVATION TO PROPEL YOURSELF TO SUCCESS

Ace McCloud

LOSE WEIGHT

THE TOP 100 BEST WAYS TO LOSE WEIGHT QUICKLY AND HEALTHILY

Ace McCloud

SELF DISCIPLINE

Unleash The Power Of Self Discipline, Influence And Willpower In Your Life To Achieve Anything

Ace McCloud

Ace McCloud

HABIT

The Top 100 Best Habits
How To Make A Positive Habit Permanent
And How To Break Bad Habits

ATTITUDE

Discover The True Power Of A Positive Attitude

Ace McCloud

ULTIMATE HEALTH SECRETS

HEALTH

Strategies For Dieting, Eating Healthy, Exercising,
Losing Weight, The Mediterranean Diet,
Strength Training, And All About Vitamins,
Minerals, And Supplements

Ace McCloud

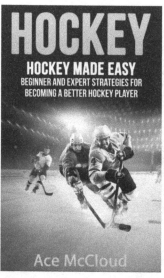

HOCKEY

HOCKEY MADE EASY
BEGINNER AND EXPERT STRATEGIES FOR
BECOMING A BETTER HOCKEY PLAYER

Ace McCloud

Be sure to check out my audio books as well!

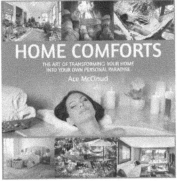

Check out my website at: www.AcesEbooks.com for a complete list of all of my books and high quality audio books. I enjoy bringing you the best knowledge in the world and wish you the best in using this information to make your journey through life better and more enjoyable! **Best of luck to you!**

CPSIA information can be obtained
at www.ICGtesting.com
Printed in the USA
BVHW081110121118
532890BV00010B/500/P